# The People Who Tested God

Will man rob God? Yet you are robbing me. But you say, 'How are we robbing thee?' In your tithes and offerings. You are cursed with a curse, for you are robbing me; the whole nation of you. Bring the full tithes into the storehouse, that there may be food in my house; and thereby *put me to the test, says the* Lord *of hosts*, if I will not open the windows of heaven for you and pour down for you an overflowing blessing. I will rebuke the devourer for you, so that it will not destroy the fruits of your soil; and your vine in the field shall not fail to bear, says the Lord of hosts. Then all nations will call you blessed, for you will be a land of delight, says the Lord of hosts.

Malachi 3:8-12

## The People Who Tested God

"A young couple — she's a secretary, he's a recent college graduate just beginning a career — stopped Darrell Rickard and me in the hall the Sunday of the collection. 'We don't have much,' the young man said, 'but we want to be a part of this.' His wife handed me a small bundle containing rings, a necklace, and other items of jewelry. The jewelry had obviously been well taken care of, and as the young woman handed it to me, there were tears in her eyes. I wanted to give them back to her, tried to tell her it was their spirit we wanted, but her mind was made up. An appraiser valued the jewelry at $300, but perhaps few gifts were more precious."

Extraordinary people make extraordinary things happen. This book is the story of a people of special faith, like this young couple. And how, with God's help, they took a big risk and did a very special thing.

### THE $2 MILLION SUNDAY
### With "How To" Details

This first-of-its-kind program explains the details of how the Broadway Church of Christ raised $2,260,000 — nearly three times its annual budget — in a single-Sunday collection.

Highlights of the program include:

1) **Fund-raising Principles** (You must understand the four basic reasons people give before you can have a successful fund-raising effort.)

2) **Values of the Special Collection** (Two vital principles must be followed. If they are, the "special" will succeed and **will not** hinder regular giving.)

3) **The Many Methods of Giving** (This section alone is worth thousands of dollars in the collection plate. Carefully researched and written, this presentation, including examples, has been prepared in accordance with the Tax Form Act of 1976. An extremely valuable section.)

4) **A New Concept In Giving** (The backbone of the program, this new concept was called by one of the nation's leading fund-raisers, "the simplest, most revolutionary church fund-raising method I've ever seen.")

5) **Special Articles** (25 brief, to-the-point articles on stewardship by Joe Barnett — highly useful for church papers, letters, and sermons.)

6) **Sermons** (8 sermons by Joe Barnett on cassette tapes. Messages on stewardship, which Barnett preached in setting the stage for the "special.")

This program does not offer theoretical advice. Joe Barnett believes any church can raise one to three times its annual budget in a single-Sunday offering. In this program, he shares the "how to" details.

For further information write: GROW, Inc.
1511 Bryan Street
Dallas, TX 75201

# The People Who Tested God

## JOE R. BARNETT

**SWEET PUBLISHING COMPANY**

Austin     Texas

The People Who Tested God



Library of Congress Catalog Card Number 79-83538
ISBN 0-8344-0105-3

## Dedication

To my elders —
>... men — who because they are men —
make mistakes but are big enough
to admit them, correct them, and
aggressively lead into expanded
areas of service;
>... men of exemplary faith, determined
direction, an unfaltering vision;
>... men who love God, the people they
lead, and the lost;
>... men who are heaven-bound and are
influencing me and thousands of
others to make the journey with
them.

— Joe Barnett

# Contents

# Foreword

The Broadway Church of Christ in Lubbock, Texas attracted a good deal of attention recently when it raised more than $2 million in a single contribution, the largest single-Sunday contribution ever given by any church in the United States. It is indeed a remarkable accomplishment.

Yet, having served as Broadway's minister from 1963 until 1968, I know that the record setting contribution is solidly within the Broadway tradition. For almost a century, the Broadway Church has been accomplishing great things. Pioneer church on the Texas South Plains, a leader in mission fields around the world, founder of a child-care institution, Broadway is known nationwide for its professionalism and innovative approaches and is enthusiastically involved in ministering to Lubock's many college students. The Broadway Church continues to build on its rich heritage.

When Lubbock's earliest settlers — including Broadway's founders — journeyed to the vast, open spaces of the Texas panhandle to start a new life, they were keenly aware that mere survival would not be easy. There was land, and plenty of it; but it was harsh, and water was scarce. That they survived, indeed prospered, is a tribute both to their stubbornness and to their willingness to work incredibly hard.

The Broadway Church is imbued with that same tenacious frontier spirit; and through the years, that spirit has manifested itself in numerous ways. During the Depression, for example, the Broadway congregation of 175 families built an auditorium that seated 1,000. It was filled in 1950. An 800-member congregation built the present 2,200-seat auditorium. It, too, was soon filled.

Examples abound. In 1946, Broadway became the first religious group to send missionaries to war-torn Germany. Even before the war was over, Broadway's leaders were laying plans to preach the Word and offer much needed food and clothing to that devastated country. Broadway won the admiration of religious leaders and government officials on both continents and served as a model for missionary effort in Europe by other religious groups.

In the 1950's, Broadway's leadership started the Children's Home of Lubbock, the first child-care facility in the Southwest to utilize cottage care, instead of the dormitory approach. Since its opening in 1954, the home has served more than 1,650 children.

What distinguishes the Broadway Church above all else, it seems to me, is the quality of its leadership. Over the years, its elders have been vigorous, hardworking men with courage to lead their people into previously uncharted areas of service. They have also taken great pains to hire ministers of vision and foresight, men who can aspire the congregation to even greater accomplishments.

Since 1968, Broadway's minister has been Joe Barnett, a bright, sensitive man with an uncommon gift for motivating people. Joe Barnett is not only a man of vision, but he knows how to get things done. And in this book, he shares some of the planning and strategy that made Broadway's special contribution a success. He discusses church-arranged loans, deferred giving, and the other innovative techniques that Broadway used to further the Lord's work. He also shares a bit of this congregation's proud history and discusses the guiding philosophy that undergirds the activities of the church.

It's an inspiring story about an unusual congregation in this era of spiritual poverty, crumbling values, and a preternatural preoccupation with the self. It's refreshing to read about a people willing to share their prosperity, willing to sacrifice; a people with an eye to serving their fellowman and sharing God's love; a people with a deep commitment to the sanctity of home, family, and to the church that Jesus died to save. Like a "city set on a hill," this congregation on the Texas plains can be for all of us a shining example and a beacon of hope.

William Slater Banowsky
President
The University of Oklahoma

# 1

# The Challenge to Give

On November 19, 1978, the Broadway Church of Christ in Lubbock, Texas contributed more than $2.4 million to the Lord's work, the largest single church collection in United States history. Along with $1.65 million in cash or soon to be paid pledges, the collection plates that morning were filled to overflowing, so to speak, with jewelry, a house, a teenager's guitar, a pecan orchard, two lots in Ruidoso, New Mexico — and a five-year-old's 'Big Wheel.'

More than $300,000 was contributed by sixteen elders, an average of about $21,000 each; the elders, deacons, and staff together pledged three-quarters of a million dollars. Junior high school students had set a goal of $1,250; they raised $1,905. Senior high students surpassed their goal of $10,000 with gifts of $10,208. More than $144,000 was given in nickels, dimes, quarters, and small bills, an indication that Broadway children had been saving for the special collection and that their parents had been putting back dollars and extra change anticipating this special day. The largest individual gift was $70,000.

The record-breaking contribution also included numerous deferred gifts, primarily through inclusion in wills. The deferred gifts amount to a conservative estimate of approximately $500,000.

To a country boy from West Texas, $2.4 million is a breathtakingly large sum, but as Los Angeles *Times* Religion Writer John Dart pointed out recently, religious groups across the country are raising record amounts of money in one-time special contributions. "It doesn't have the drama of a Pete Rose consecutive-game batting streak," Dart writes, "but let it be noted that the unofficial record for the most money slipped into a church's collection plates on a single Sunday has been broken four times in the last fourteen months."

That was in July. Four months after Dart's article, the Broadway Church nudged the record even higher.

The previous record-holder, according to John Dart, was the independent Overlake Christian Church in the Seattle suburb of Kirkland. The 1,700-member congregation attempted to meet the projected cost of $1.8 million to build a new auditorium. Their single Sunday offering in June of 1978 amounted to $1,650,000 in gifts, cash, pledges, and deferred payments.

The Overlake Christian Church donations — which included seven diamond rings, several vehicles, and newly borrowed money — came only one Sunday after the Garden Grove, California Community Church and its ebullient minister Robert Schuller claimed the record on June 18.

Dropped into hardhats and wheelbarrows at the Orange County drive-in/walk-in church that day was $1,251,000. After opening the next days' mail from people who could not attend, church officials said the to-

# RECORD SUNDAY CHURCH COLLECTIONS

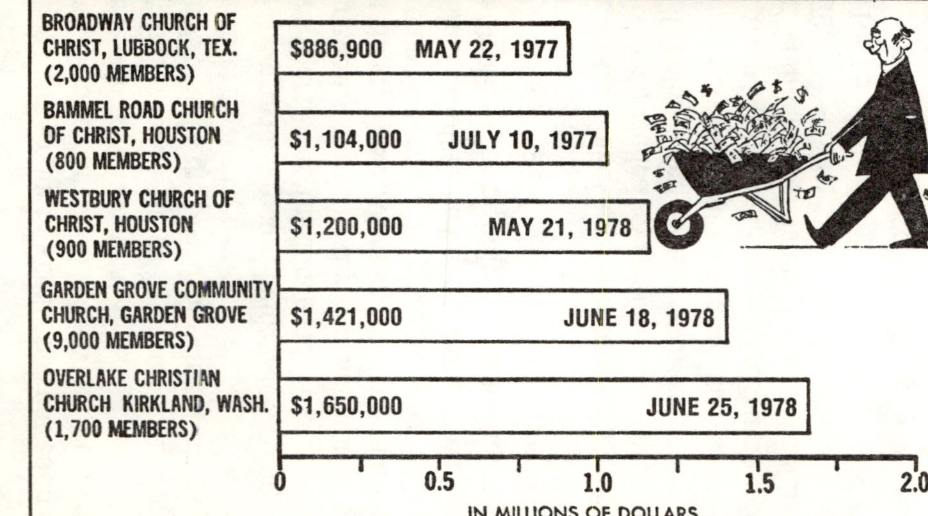

tal ran to $1,421,000 — well over the amount needed to make a payment deadline on the church's Crystal Cathedral now under construction.

Previous high single-day contributions were reported by three Church of Christ congregations in Texas. On May 22, 1977 — about eighteen months prior to our 1978 record-breaker — we here at Broadway raised $886,900. Two months later, the Bammel Road Church in Houston raised $1,104,000, and in May of 1978 Houston's Westbury Church of Christ raised $1,200,000.

The unofficial world champion, however, must be the 1,000-member Glad Tidings Temple in Vancouver, British Columbia. On September 10, 1978, this Pentecostal church, affiliated with the worldwide Revival Fellowship, garnered $2,014,000 in cash or pledged commitments of time payments. It was reported that a Brinks armored car with its motor running waited outside the church building.

As more and more churches turn to the special contribution as an effective money-raising technique, the Broadway mark will doubtless be surpassed — perhaps by Broadway herself — but engaging in what we might call Collection Plate Olympics is not what sacrificial giving is all about. Here at Broadway we desperately needed a new educational building; because of the sky-high interest rates that prevail these days, we needed to go into that building debt-free when it is completed in 1980. The $2 1/2 million special contribution puts us well on the way toward reaching our $3.8 million goal, and as our people continue to make sacrificial gifts and pledges over the next two years, we have every reason to believe we'll make it.

But that's not all. As Joe Schubert, minister of the Bammel Road Church in Houston, has pointed out, "Special contributions help rather than hinder the regular weekly collections because giving is a trait of character that is learned." We learn to give, in other words, by giving.

According to Schubert, a questionnaire handed out several weeks after Bammel Road's record-setting fund-raiser showed that ninety-four percent of the respondents thought the drive had a beneficial effect on their spiritual life. Ninety-one percent indi-

cated their willingness to do it again sometime. "There is little doubt they will receive
that opportunity," Schubert wrote in a recent *Gospel Advocate* article.

Here at Broadway, we discovered the
same thing. Numerous people dropped notes
into the collection plate on that November
morning saying, in effect, "Thank you for finally giving us the oportunity to give, for
challenging us to say 'Unless we really sacrifice, we're not going to make it.' " Contributions since November 19 have also been extremely good. One Sunday in December, for
example, the contribution came to $38,000;
our weekly budget is $17,000.

In effect, we are teaching people how to
give, and I am compelled to believe what
God says about giving — that to give is to be
blessed in return. The soaring words of Jesus as recorded in Luke 6 are appropriate —
particularly for an agricultural region like
ours: ". . . give, and it will be given to you:
good measure, pressed down, shaken together, running over, will be put into your
lap. For the measure you give will be the
measure you get back" (v. 38).

That has been my experience, and the experience of everyone I know. And because I want the people at Broadway to be blessed, I emphasize the importance of giving.

But to give, of course, also requires sacrifice, and that is another valuable lesson we at Broadway are learning. A week before our special contribution, a woman came by the office to explain that she and her husband wanted very much to be one of the 250 families we were urging to commit themselves to a $4,000 gift — which would total a million dollars. "But we just don't have the money," she explained, "and we've tried to figure out how we could do it."

She reached into her purse and pulled out several photographs of one of the most beautiful antique beds I've ever seen. Over a hundred years old, rosewood trimmed in walnut with a headboard that reached the ceiling, it was a magnificently crafted piece of furniture. "We've decided to sell this bed," she said.

I looked at those pictures for a long time. I ached inside at the thought of her giving up a family treasure, and yet I knew she would be blessed by making the sacrifice. I told her how I felt. "Well, I don't want to sell it either," she said, and then she honed in on a basic truth we would all at times rather avoid. "I've decided," she said, "that you haven't really given until you've given up something that you desperately want to keep. And I want to keep that bed worse than anything I've got."

She pledged the bed, making the same hard choice as the man who dropped his watch into the collection plate that Sunday morning. "This watch means a lot to me," he wrote on the contribution envelope, "and this is what I want to give." Many others made similar decisions, including two high school students who took out thousand dollar loans which they will pay back working part time over the next couple of years.

What we are learning from our special contribution, from our sacrificial giving, is the lesson Dietrich Bonhoeffer wrote about in *The Cost of Discipleship:* "Earthly goods are given to be used," Bonhoeffer wrote, "not to be collected. In the wilderness God gave Israel the manna every day, and they had no need to worry about food and drink. Indeed, if they kept any of the manna over until the next day, it went bad. In the same way, the disciple must receive his portion from God every day. If he stores it up as a permanent possession, he spoils not only the gift, but himself as well, for he sets his heart on his accumulated wealth, and makes it a barrier between himself and God. Where our treasure is, there is our trust, our security, our consolation and our God. Hoarding is idolatry."

Was I surprised, people have asked, at the amount of the contribution? I was pleased, I tell them in all candor, but not surprised. The Broadway Church has been a pioneering congregation since that day in 1890 when forty people journeyed by covered wagon to the desolate, sparsely populated South Plains of Texas to start a new life and establish a congregation of the Lord's people. The first Church of Christ in West Texas and eastern New Mexico, a leader in mission work, one of the first to establish a college Bible chair, a pioneer in the field of child care, a strong advocate of Christian higher education — the Broadway Church of Christ has been "testing God" for nearly nine decades. The November 19 special contribution is only the latest pioneering effort.

The local church is the primary instrument of our Lord to bring the gospel to the souls of men. For two thousand years the local church has been the launching pad for evangelism and Christian training. For nearly a century, the Broadway Church has been in this business. What has set Broadway apart over the years has been its willingness to use fresh, innovative methods like the special contribution to tell the "old, old story" — that, and the quality of its leadership. Leaders of the Broadway congregation — its elders, ministers, deacons, and teachers — always have been blessed with great vision; its ministers have traditionally been leaders, not just in the community, but in the brotherhood at large. The special contribution must be seen in the context of this rich tradition.

Perhaps Reuel Lemmons put it best in a 1967 issue of *Firm Foundation* focusing on Lubbock churches: "No claim is made that all of the revolutionary ideas among the Lubbock churches are the best decisions or that no mistakes have been made in some of the projects undertaken. However, the broad range of works in which Lubbock churches have taken the lead is some indication of the quality of vision, zeal and dedication among the leadership."

In short, Broadway has been a richly blessed congregation. As we once again affirmed on November 19, our blessings increase our responsibility. We praise God for everything that has been accomplished, and we thank him for opportunities yet to come.

# 2

# The Challenge to Decide

Twenty-eight years ago, the Broadway Church dedicated a building its minister described as "simple, majestic . . . with beautiful lines but not ornate, an instrument to help us in worship, not a monument to be worshipped itself."

"We spared no expense in our effort to erect a permanent building," Dr. Norvel Young continued, "but we made it plain and simple. Our people will come here to worship God, not to revel in the beauty of our building."

The handsome new three-story building, completed after two years of construction and a decade of planning, featured a 2,200-seat auditorium, a chapel accomodating 300, offices, and classrooms. Total cost was approximately $1 million. It was the largest, most expensive building any Church of Christ had ever built. "We hope the building will stand for hundreds of years," Dr. Young told a reporter.

With its light buff brick and red tile roof, Broadway's building is still a handsome edifice, one of several impressive church buildings lining the city's main street between downtown Lubbock and the Texas Tech University campus. It has served us well and continues to do so, but as we moved into the 1970's, we were feeling the need for more space. It had been built by a membership of about 800; twenty years later, we were approaching 3,000. With two Sunday-morning services, our auditorium could accomodate the growth, but our classrooms had reached their limit.

A decision had to be made, not simply a decision about brick and mortar — but about souls. Would we continue to grow and serve and evangelize? Would we continue to play a vital role in this community? Or would we

rest on our proud history and let someone else do God's work? Younger, more energetic congregations perhaps.

Toward the end of 1972, the Broadway elders set in motion the most comprehensive planning effort I've ever seen, an effort that culminated in the events of November 19, 1978. For six years, the Broadway elders pored over projected needs, growth patterns — particularly for the preceding decade — financial figures, and architectural plans. The mountain of information confirmed our initial opinion: unless Broadway was willing to build, we were boxing ourselves into a "no growth" future. And "no growth" we realized, usually means not just stasis but eventual decline.

What we needed, our elders decided, was an educational building that would offer us space for large congregational fellowship meetings as well as additional classroom space. Presently we have classroom space for approximately 1,500; our new building will accomodate another 2,000. Price tag for our needs — $3,806,376.

---

## DEVELOPMENTS TO DATE

- December, 1972
    Elders appointed committee to study building needs of the church regarding:
    Proposals and costs
    Feasibility of building and/or remodeling
    Initial conceptual drawings
    Timing of building (and phases)
    Possible means of financing
- March, 1973
    Presentation of staff studies showing continued growth dependent upon expansion of facilities.
- November, 1974
    Preliminary committee report to elders outlining present, future and long-range needs.
- March, 1975
    Initial program studies presented to deacons.

- September, 1975

    Preliminary concepts to meet program needs presented to elders. Selection of architects authorized.

- January, 1976

    Architects selected by elders.

- April, 1976

    Architects presented several concepts of building expansion program. Decision made to proceed with schematic drawings for approval.

- August, 1976

    Completed schematics presented to elders. Elders asked committee to proceed in development of financial plan.

- November, 1976

    Decision made to present program to congregation on December 19.

- December 19, 1976

    Presentation to congregation.

---

The need was obvious, but the decision to build was painfully slow in coming. Despite years of planning and research, despite the obvious need, the eighteen men who lead this congregation agonized over their decision. Dedicated men, sincere in their convictions, some were still reluctant to commit the congregation to a program so expensive they

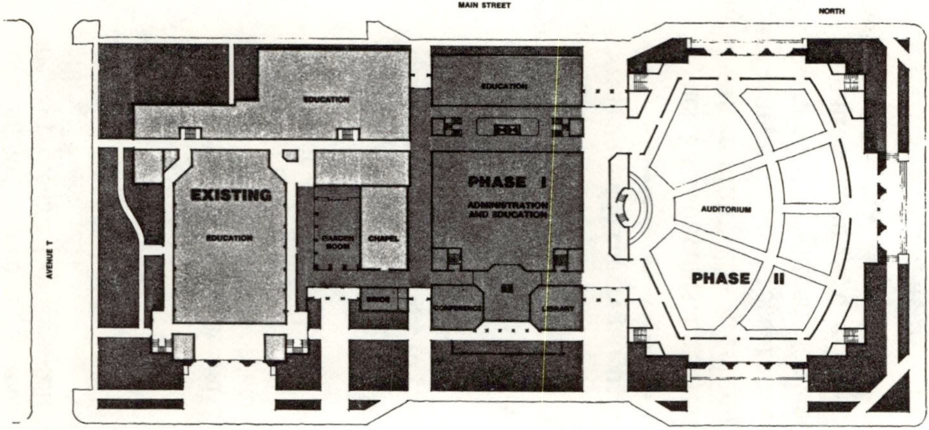


LONG RANGE DEVELOPMENT PLAN

might not live long enough to see it fulfilled. As responsible stewards, they just did not feel right about burdening future generations. As we temporized, however, we were in danger of bypassing a peak period of opportunity. Like the person who must examine every alternative before taking a step, we were spending an unconscionably long time with one foot in the air.

We were facing another problem as well. That unity so characteristic of the Broadway leadership — and so vital to any congregation's success — was in danger of unraveling. Second thoughts, comments about building an unneeded building began to surface, the kind of comments that nourish self-fulfilling prophecies. Broadway had never built a building that it didn't grow to fill; but always before the leadership had taken a strongly aggressive position, and the people happily followed.

Like most pioneers, the Broadway Church over the years has received its share of criticism — both from within the congregation and from the outside. Opposing viewpoints have always been carefully, thoughtfully considered by the Broadway leadership, but once a consensus is reached, dissenters are not permitted to create problems — or to prevail. Among the leaders themselves, discussion, debate, even serious differences of opinion characterize most decisions — which is natural when eighteen men lead 3,000 people. But once the decision is made, the Broadway elders traditionally close ranks and present a united front. One of Broadway's strengths, in other words, is that neither inside nor outside critics have been able to intimidate the congregation's leaders. They have been strong men. Norvel Young says it has something to do with the frontier spirit that characterized the South Plain's not-so-distant past. Whatever the reason, Broadway's leaders have been decisive — not arrogant or stubborn, but decisive.

This building program, however, came closer to precipitating division among our elders than anything they've ever done. We had some very influential people in this church who fought the program and fought it hard. Facing a great deal of pressure, our elders came dangerously close to letting something happen that would have been unprecedented. Backing off, giving in, looked very tempting.

After the 800-member Bammel Road congregation in Houston raised $1.1 million in a special collection in 1977, its elders surveyed those who participated to see what factors had most influenced them to respond. Nine separate items were mentioned, including sermons from the pulpit, all-night prayer sessions, and dinner meetings where the fund drive was explained. The most important factor, however, was the example of elders, deacons, and staff; their sacrificed gifts and their unity.

As Bammel Road minister Joe Schubert points out in a book edited by James Vinzant called the *The Special Contribution*, "It is interesting to observe that the very thing that the church has always been hesitant about doing — that is, letting the church know what someone is giving — was the very thing that was the most influential in getting the members to participate. It seems that when we grow to a spiritual level where we can share our giving amounts that the whole church will be benefitted. This was the number one motivation. This should be done deliberately and without apology. The congregation must know where the leaders stand." (p. 19)

Broadway's elders eventually stepped forward in a magnificent way, but for a frustratingly long time, the Broadway congregation could not gauge where its leaders stood on this program. However, the measure of the men is seen in the fact that Broadway's elders, in characteristic style, eventually stepped forward in a magnificent way.

I fondly remember Alex McDonald, a long-time Broadway elder who died in 1973. I recall a meeting where Alex was arguing against a program that most of his colleagues supported — Alex was the watchdog of the treasury when it came to considering programs that cost money — and he was arguing with passion and some force. The vote went against Alex. Alex McDonald's first comment after the vote was 'If we're gonna do it, let's get on with it. Let me make the announcement tonight about what we want to do.' Anyone listening to Alex that night would have believed Alex McDonald thought up the idea, pushed through the program against all odds, and was never anything less than a hundred percent behind it.

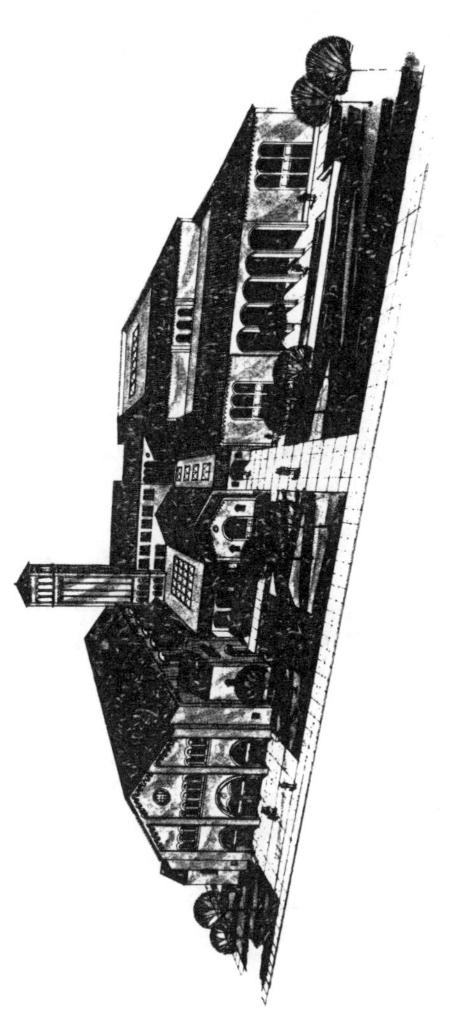

VIEW FROM BROADWAY

Although it took a while, the spirit of Alex McDonald finally prevailed in this decision too. One factor that moved us off high center was the enthusiasm of several younger elders who were willing to shoulder the responsibility for Broadway's future. In the words of one of them, "Those of us who moved in here the last twenty years really hadn't done much but enjoy the facilities already here. But you can't keep dipping out of the bucket indefinitely. Now it's our turn to do something for our children that they can enjoy the next twenty years."

So the elders made their decision, and with that decision came the glimmer of an idea. It was an idea with well known biblical precedents when it came to building things. When the Israelites built the tabernacle, for instance, "they came, everyone whose heart stirred him, and every one whose spirit moved him, and brought the Lord's offering to be used for the tent of meeting, and for all its service, and for the holy garments. So they came, both men and women; all who were of a willing heart brought brooches and earrings and signet rings and armlets, all sorts of gold objects, every man dedicating an offering of gold to the Lord . . . All the men and women, the people of Israel, whose heart moved them to bring anything for the work which the Lord had commanded by Moses to be done, brought it as their freewill offering to the Lord" (Exodus 35:21-22, 29). The workers eventually told Moses " 'The people bring much more than enough for doing the work which the Lord has commanded us to do' . . . So the people were restrained from bringing; for the stuff they had was sufficient to do all the work, and more" (Exodus 36:5-7).

Many years later, the people of Israel, responding to the desire of King David to build a temple, "gave for the service of the house of God five thousand talents and ten thousand darics of gold, ten thousand talents of silver, eighteen thousand talents of bronze, and a hundred thousand talents of iron. And whoever had precious stones gave them to the treasury of the house of the Lord, in the care of Jehiel the Gershonite. Then the people rejoiced because these had given willingly, for with a whole heart they had offered freely to the Lord; David the king also rejoiced greatly" (1 Chronicles 29:7-9).

Like the Israelites of old building their tabernacle, like David's people bringing their offerings "with a whole heart" to build the temple, why not pay cash for our building, thus avoiding those crippling mortgage and interest payments? But pay cash for a $3.8 million building? Was it foolish to even think about going into that building debt-free? Was there any way to do it? How would our people respond?

We had to have the building, there was no longer any question, and yet interest alone on $4 million is half our annual budget. If we carried heavy mortgage and interest payments with us into that building, we would be forced to cut back on benevolence and mission work: at the very least, we will be unable to expand these works.

"If we have to cut back on our mission work, I'm not in favor of building that building, " I told our elders. "If we have to cut back on our benevolent work, I'm not in favor of building that building. But if we can go into it debt-free, then I think we ought to do it.'

The more I thought about it, the more convinced I became that there might be a way.

3

# The Challenge to Innovate

"When Joe started talking about moving into that building debt-free, I just kind of thought he'd lost his marbles," J. B. Mc-Corkle, one of our elders, told me laughingly a few days ago. What Dr. McCorkle, a man of great vision, along with the rest of us at Broadway, soon realized, however, was that much more effective ways of fund-raising than we had ever really considered could be put to use for the Lord.

From May through November, we explained these giving options to our members at monthly meetings we called Church Nights. At each meeting, a segment of the congregation — usually between 160 and 170 adults — would come together to learn how they would be able to make gifts larger than they ever dreamed possible.

Each Church Night followed the same format. After a buffet meal in the fellowship hall, I welcomed those attending, then showed a multi-media presentation of Broadway's history and future plans. Next Dr. McCorkle, on behalf of the elders, explained what we were hoping to accomplish with our special contribution. After a discussion of the contribution options, we closed with a song and prayer. By November every member had been invited, and a large majority had participated.

Perhaps the most innovative plan we discussed on those Church Nights involved the church-arranged loan. This plan is based on two factors Americans use extensively to achieve desired possessions: the ability of ordinary working people to borrow money, and the existence in our industrial society of dependable, regular incomes. These two elements are basic to our economy. We use them to fund houses, appliances, furniture, cars, education, businesses, even vacations.

We borrow money, and we pay off the loan through regular payments to the lending institution. This is the system we have adopted in this country to meet financial obligations which at one time we would have considered prohibitive. Since we use this method to finance our needs — and luxuries — why shouldn't we be willing to use the same plan to provide for God's work?

We used the church-arranged loan for our special contribution in May, 1977; as far as we know, we were the first church to do so. Doug Lawson, an extremely knowledgable New York City fund-raiser, called the method "revolutionary." According to Lawson, who put together Bob Schuller's $20 million Crystal Cathedral campaign, the church-arranged loan will be used as extensively for churches as the practice of selling bonds has been in the past.

To set up the loan plan, we went to several Lubbock banks and explained that we wanted to make it possible for our people to borrow money to give to this program and then pay it back over a specified period of time, preferably up to four years. We also requested that the banks loan to *any* member of this church who wanted to borrow, with no financial statements required.

It was necessary, of course, to find lending institutions willing to loan to every family in the congregation. Since there were some families with limited or non-existent borrowing ability, the church itself was essentially guaranteeing the loan. If any of our members default — and none have — the church will pay off the note. But since the church got the money in the first place, we are taking no financial risk.

Five Lubbock banks agreed to cooperate with the May, 1977 contribution; seven with the November, 1978 drive. The church-arranged loan was a key to our success that first time, but we didn't use the loan plan as effectively as we might have. For our November 19 drive, we set out to eliminate the kinks.

The most obvious drawback was that our members still had to visit their bank, sign the note, and then get the money. I wanted to arrange it so that the borrower never had to visit the bank; I wanted to make it just as simple as possible.

After numerous complications, we finally

# MONTHLY LOAN PAYBACK SCHEDULE

| amount borrowed | four years or 48 months | three years or 36 months | two years or 24 months |
|---|---|---|---|
| $ 500 | $ | $ 16.38 | $ 23.33 |
| 1,000 | 25.83 | 32.77 | 46.66 |
| 1,500 | 38.75 | 49.16 | 70.00 |
| 2,000 | 51.66 | 65.55 | 93.33 |
| 2,500 | 64.58 | 81.94 | 116.66 |
| 3,000 | 77.50 | 98.33 | 140.00 |
| 4,000 | 103.33 | 131.11 | 186.67 |
| 5,000 | 129.17 | 163.89 | 233.33 |
| 7,500 | 193.75 | 245.78 | 350.00 |
| 10,000 | 258.34 | 327.77 | 466.66 |
| 12,000 | 309.96 | 393.30 | 560.00 |
| 15,000 | 387.45 | 491.60 | 700.00 |
| 20,000 | 516.60 | 655.50 | 933.30 |
| 25,000 | 645.75 | 819.40 | 1,166.60 |
| 30,000 | 774.90 | 983.30 | 1,400.00 |
| 40,000 | 1,033.20 | 1,311.10 | 1,866.60 |
| 50,000 | 1,291.50 | 1,638.80 | 2,333.30 |
| 60,000 | 1,549.80 | 1,966.60 | 2,800.00 |
| 75,000 | 1,937.25 | 2,458.30 | 3,500.00 |
| 80,000 | 2,066.40 | 2,622.20 | 3,733.30 |
| 90,000 | 2,324.70 | 2,950.00 | 4,200.00 |
| 100,000 | 2,583.00 | 3,277.70 | 4,666.60 |

arranged with the seven banks a plan whereby our members had only to sign a card on November 19 stating the amount he or she wanted to borrow and how long they wanted to take paying it back. A pay-back schedule was provided with the card. We in turn told the bank how much the individual wanted to borrow. The bank would then mail the note to the borrower, the borrower would sign the note, and the bank would issue a cashier's check directly to the church.

The church-arranged loan made it possible for us to focus on a specific dollar figure — $4,000. If we could encourage 250 of our families to each give $4,000, that would be a million dollars to start with. We believed that many of our families could handle that amount, and on the bank pay-back schedule, it was the closest figure to $100 a month ($103.33 a month over 48 months).

Along with the church-arranged loan, we emphasized gifts of personal and real property. Since most of us are not very creative in our giving, we focused on specifics. To be able to say, "Here is a person who gave a car, here's a person who gave a farm, this person gave a year's salary," starts people to thinking. "I didn't think I could give anything, but maybe I can," they say to themselves. "Maybe I *do* have something to give." And that's when the orchards, the jewelry, and the houses, began rolling in.

We were also careful to explain how these gifts of real and personal property to the Broadway Church made the donor eligible to receive a charitable deduction from his income tax for the year in which the gift is made. And we explained how a double tax saving may be possible when donating gifts such as securities, real estate or other property which (1) are deemed to be capital assets in the hands of the donor; (2) have been held by the donor for at least twelve months; (3) have increased in value since the donor's acquisition. (A planned giving brochure distributed by the Broadway Church entitled "Opportunities for Giving to Benefit: The Church, Your Family, Your Estate, and You" discussed these options in some detail.)

Another fund-raising option we began to use during this campaign involves deferred giving. Over half of all the capital gifts made in this country are deferred gifts. Our colleges and some of our children's homes take advantage of this method, and it should be a viable option for churches as well.

At Broadway, for instance, seventy-eight percent of the elders put the church in their wills during this program. Several of our deacons, most of our ministers, and several members did the same thing. Others bought insurance policies with the church as beneficiary. A conservative estimate of $500,000 has been placed on deferred gift expectancies.

A testamentary gift, it seems to me, is another form of responsible stewardship. We all realize that the government gets a great deal of money that could go to churches, and a carefully considered will allows an individual to continue giving even after his death. Consider, for example, a man who has been a part of the Broadway Church since he was a small boy. Perhaps he is an elder now or a deacon, and for years he's poured his life into this church. Given a choice, he would much rather the church get his money when he dies instead of the government.

Of course, that man *does* have a choice. But if he does not put this church — or some other good work for that matter — in his will, then the state writes his will for him, and the state gets most of the money.

The federal and state governments have long recognized the desirability of encouraging gifts to educational and other institutions serving the public interest. That's why federal and state laws (including the Tax Reform Act of 1976) provide numerous incentives for taxpayers to make immediate and deferred gifts to qualified institutions such as the Broadway Church. During our Church Nights we emphasized the attractive opportunities available to donors for present and deferred gifts that provide definite tax advantages. We also pointed out that each gift could be tailored to the donor's specific tax situation and his family's specific long and short term financial needs and plans.

There was much to talk about, and much of it rather complex, but as we moved into November we were asked to announce the clear and tangible support of our elders — an absolutely vital element, as Joe Schubert pointed out, in Bammel Road's success and in ours as well.

The first time our sixteen elders (two

other elders are incapacitated by illness) made their commitments, their total came to approximately $250,000. Frankly, I felt we weren't going to make it without more from our leadership. I respectfully asked them to reconsider what they believed they were able to do, pointing out that strictly from a fund-raising point of view I believed it mandatory that our leadership give more, and then left the room. When their revamped commitments came in a bit later, the results were astounding. Some had doubled their contribution, at least one had quadrupled. The figure came to $327,000, an average of something over $21,000 per man.

After the elders had reworked their commitment, they challenged the deacons to reconsider theirs — which they did — so that by November 19, our leadership — elders, deacons, and staff — had already committed three-quarters of a million dollars. That was our seed money.

One of the keys to our leadership support, I am convinced, was our successful effort to pinpoint one man to function as a ''leader's leader,'' one man — whom he would be we didn't know — who would be challenged to dig even deeper than any of the others, thus serving as a symbol of what one person could do. We found the man we thought would be ideal, a man already committed to the building program who had given substantially in our 1977 special contribution. Over lunch one day, two of our ministers explained what they had in mind. The figure they suggested was three times the amount he had given in May, 1977. "He got very quiet," Darrell Rickard, one of the ministers recalls. "For five minutes he sat there fidgeting with the salt shaker not saying a word. Finally he looked up and said, 'I'll do it. I don't know how, but I'll do it.' "

"Boy if I'd known what you were asking me to lunch for, I don't think I would have come," he told us a few days later. He laughed. After November 19, he told me he felt good about what he had done. He said he felt as if a burden had been lifted.

That kind of thinking is what made this special contribution possible. We had to have that kind of leadership. That man talked to a great many people about supporting the program. Whether he ever told any of them how much he himself gave, I don't know; I do know that his wholehearted support and enthusiasm was so obvious after he made his commitment that he really didn't have to tell.

Throughout the year-long campaign we were also especially sensitive to timing. At Broadway we have numerous special contributions, and with each of them, there is always a danger of peaking too quickly or of failing to build enthusiasm soon enough. And we were especially concerned about following too closely on the heels of the May, 1977 contribution. We also knew that the fall of the year is the best time for meeting goals. That may be true everywhere, but because of the fall harvest and the return of our university students, it is especially true here.

Finding the right time has to do with measuring very carefully what I like to call the "climate" of the congregation, that intangible mood that emanates from all organized groups. It may be difficult to measure, but it most definitely exists.

I must be careful, for instance, to tailor my sermons to my reading of the congregational climate. I preach often on giving — because I believe people are blessed by giving — but I absolutely refuse to preach sermons designed to make people give out of guilt. The buildup for this special contribution was no different.

People can be pressured to give, of course, but they will be giving for the wrong reasons, and I do not want anyone to give unless he or she feels good about it. Otherwise, their gift does them little good, and I'm not at all sure that God receives a gift unless the person gives out of the right spirit.

Also as a matter of climate, I repeatedly explained to our people that they were not *required* to give to this program. I hope you want to, I hastened to add, but there are many good works — Lubbock Christian College, Abilene Christian University, the Children's Home, to name a few — and I realize that Broadway people are called on more than any people I know to contribute to other good works. People have a right to choose, I explained. So far, seventy percent of the members of this congregation have chosen to commit themselves to this program.

On November 6 — a couple of weeks before the big day — we held a final Church

Night at the Lubbock Civic Center, this one for the entire congregation. More than a thousand people turned out to hear a rousing talk by Dr. William S. Banowsky, Broadway's minister during the 1960's and now the President of the University of Oklahoma.

One of the most dynamic speakers in America, Banowsky discussed Broadway's unusual eighty-eight year history, pointing out the congregation's role as both a presence in the community and a model for the brotherhood. If this project were not underway, he said, Broadway would be compelled to find another because a congregation must continue to fuel its progress into the future. To keep that energy moving in positive directions, the Broadway people must continuously test their faith, Banowsky said, they must continue their willingness to risk.

Moving into our final week, things were looking good. All of us — deacons, elders, and staff — had talked to many people, and commitments were already coming in. We felt we could count on at least $1.5 million. But what should we do the week of the 12th? Darrell Rickard and I discussed our home-stretch strategy. We thought about contacting certain people and challenging them to give more, but then we decided against it. The more options we discussed the stronger grew the feeling in both of us that now it was in the Lord's hands; there was nothing else we could do. On Wednesday night the congregation held a special prayer session, and members were meeting in homes to pray together throughout the week, but Darrell and I made not one contact the whole week. The seeds had been sown; all that remained was the harvest.

4

# The Challenge to Sacrifice

Sunday, November 19 dawned sunny and pleasant in Lubbock, and as people gathered for our first services I detected a feeling of readiness — not excitement so much as a quiet kind of resolve. They had made up their minds apparently, and today was the day merely to ratify what had already been decided. Some people were no doubt wondering, "Why am I giving this much?" but most seemed to have come prepared. Attendance was very good at both services.

After our song service, a prayer, and the Lord's Supper, I gave a brief lesson, and then we handed out the brochures that out-

# My Commitment To Our Building Program

Cash or check (enclose in envelope) . . . . . . . . . . . . . . . . . . . . . . . . . . . . . . . . . . . . . . . . . . . . . . . . . . . . . . . . . . . (Amount) $ _____________

Real Estate . . . . . . . . . . . . . . . . . . . . . . . . . . . . . . . . . . . . . . . . . . . . . . . . . . . . . . . . . . . . . . . . . . . . . (Value) $ _____________

Stocks and/or bonds . . . . . . . . . . . . . . . . . . . . . . . . . . . . . . . . . . . . . . . . . . . . . . . . . . . . . . . . . . . . . . (Value) $ _____________

Other . . . . . . . . . . . . . . . . . . . . . . . . . . . . . . . . . . . . . . . . . . . . . . . . . . . . . . . . . . . . . . . . . . . . . . . . . . . . . (Value) $ _____________

I (we) desire to make my (our) gift through a church arranged loan in the amount of . . . . . . . . . . $ _____________

    Loan Information:

1. Bank preference (check one)
   - ☐ First National
   - ☐ Lubbock National
   - ☐ American State
   - ☐ Bank of the West
   - ☐ Plains National Bank
   - ☐ Security National Bank
   - ☐ Texas Bank

2. Number of months desired for payback:
   - ☐ 12 months
   - ☐ 24 months
   - ☐ 36 months
   - ☐ 48 months

3. I used the Bank Loan arrangement in the previous drive. I want to renew the unpaid balance of that loan for an additional $____________, the total amount to be paid over ____________ months.

4. Desired day of month for payment ____________

, (we) desire to make an additional deferred gift through:
- ☐ a gift of property
- ☐ a bargain sale . . . . . . . . . . . . . . . . . . . . . . . . . . . . . . . . . . . . . . . . $ _____________
- ☐ a charitable remainder annuity trust
- ☐ a charitable remainder unitrust
- ☐ life insurance
- ☐ life income agreement
- ☐ will

_______________________________  
(Signature)

Total Gift $ _____________

lined our needs. We asked that each person fill out the commitment card and insert it, along with his or her gift, in the envelope provided.

Between morning services I could feel the excitement growing. People talked eagerly among themselves on the way to classes, speculating about how we had done. During Bible class there was an undercurrent of excitement. And the presence of two police cars parked outside added to the feeling that something special was happening. (Police officers were requested because our special collection had become known all over town.) The second service was a replay of the first, and that afternoon we began to get some idea of what we had accomplished.

All afternoon men with adding machines and calculators sat at tables counting and tabulating in Darrell Rickard's office. As time for the evening service drew near, they had reached a fairly firm figure, but they felt a recount was necessary, mainly because some of the property and deferred gift commitments were difficult to interpret. We had never mentioned a specific amount we were shooting for; all I had said from the pulpit was "We can pay for this building."

Just before evening service began, I was handed a note with the dollar amount. The audience was buzzing. Looks of expectancy lit almost every face — except for the man in charge of the count. He sat with a worried frown creasing his forehead, scared to death that he might have double-figured the cash contribution. "We are close to $2 million," I announced, "and gifts are still coming in." Murmurs of approval, hearty 'amen's!', and quiet smiles of satisfaction greeted the announcement. "Our elders will be here until nine tonight," I announced, "for people who haven't given or for people who want to increase their gift." The gifts kept coming.

On Monday we recounted — the cash had not been double-figured — made estimates of jewelry and other property, and arrived at a definite figure. As of Monday afternoon, that figure stood at $2,250,000, and it was growing. Cash contributions amounted to about $800,000. Bank loans came to over $300,000. On Tuesday, the wire services picked up the story, and Paul Harvey mentioned it on his Wednesday newscast.

Wednesday night prayer meeting was the

most exciting service of all. The announcement was made that we had gone over $2 million, and then we played a tape of Paul Harvey's comments. "A record church collection at the Broadway Church of Christ in Lubbock, Texas," Harvey announced in his clipped, inimitable style. "The 3,000-member congregation has been prepared for weeks for the fact that a new education building would have to be paid for somehow, and when the collection was counted it included cash and checks and deeds to property and jewelry, a grand total one-day collection of two million dollars. Gonna be a lot of pastors citing this example to their congregations next Sunday," Harvey concluded. Our people burst into spontaneous applause. We thanked God for what we had been able to do.

Stories abound about what went into that contribution. One of our newer deacons comes to mind, a young man who attended the meeting where our elders challenged the deacons to make even more substantial commitments. He was enthusiastic, and with his wife had arrived at the amount he thought they could give. Later he attended several meetings to prepare our leadership to talk to others about the program, and he got to thinking. "My wife and I talked a long time ago about what we're going to give," he told me, "but it's just not enough. People are gonna say we're crazy, but we're upping our commitment."

Their revised commitment was three times the original.

Another deacon told me that at the time of the May, 1977 special contribution, he didn't have the money he committed, and he didn't know where he would get it. "But the Lord blessed my life," he explained. "I stepped out on faith, I worked as hard as I could, and somehow, the money was there."

This time he again doesn't know where the money is coming from, but he committed twice as much.

A young couple — she's a secretary, he's a recent college graduate just beginning a career — stopped Darrell Rickard and me in the hall the Sunday of the collection. "We don't have much," the young man said, "but we want to be a part of this." His wife handed me a small bundle containing rings, a necklace, and other items of jewelry. The jewelry had obviously been well taken care of, and as the young woman handed them to me, there were tears in her eyes. I wanted to give them back to her, tried to tell her it was their spirit we wanted, but her mind was made up. An appraiser valued the jewelry at $300, but perhaps few gifts were more precious.

I was sitting in my office one afternoon when a couple in their 70's, both on Social Security, came in and laid ten one-hundred-dollar bills on my desk. They had been saving Kennedy half dollars with silver content and some silver certificates, and the thousand dollars was the result. "It's not much," they said, "but we want it to go for that building."

Young people also caught the spirit of commitment. Senior high students took out loans. Others washed cars, mowed lawns, committed baby sitting money. Many sold some of their possessions — clothes, musical instruments, toys, whatever they could find that had any value. And the youngest of all, five-year-old Roger Guess III, gave his Big Wheel — which sold for $10 — and six cents in cash.

And so it was done. Like the Churches of

Macedonia, the Church at Lubbock "gave according to their means, of their own free will." and also like the Macedonian Churches, the Broadway Church "first gave themselves to the Lord . . ." (2 Corinthians 8:3, 5). We'll probably need one more fund drive before the new building is completed, but for now we're shifting our attention to other concerns. We realize that giving is important to the dedicated Christian, that sacrificial giving is a sign of spiritual depth, but it is not the only sign. As we move into the new year, we'll begin to emphasize other spiritual concerns — our need for each other, for example. We believe that the expression of our dependence on each other will attract others who are looking for a dedicated, loving congregation of the Lord's people. We call that "inside evangelism."

We are proud of our accomplishment, of course, but over the years there have been many accomplishments, and the Broadway Church has learned that you don't live on past glory. The Sunday night and Wednesday night after November 19 gave us ample time for self-congratulation; then it was back to work. Much is waiting to be done.

Before we talk about where Broadway goes
from here, however, it's perhaps appropriate to look at some of those past accomplishments to get some idea of where Broadway
has been.

# 5

# The Challenge of the Frontier

In the late 1880's, a plentiful supply of underground water was discovered on the dusty High Plains of Texas, and farmers began migrating to the harsh dry country looking for cheap land. Many of them headed for a raw, little community that had sprung up around a general store a hardy pioneer had opened several years before near the confluence of two military trails.

That pioneer store keeper was George W. Singer, a venturesome soul who set out in 1879 from Fort Griffin, Texas with two heavily loaded wagons along the military trail from Griffin to Fort Sumner, New Mexico.

On his wagons were lumber, a small stock of staple groceries, and other supplies. Trudging his way westward, Singer paused in Yellowstone Canyon, Lubbock County, at the point where his trail crossed the one from Fort Elliot to Fort Stockton. There was a small lake of good water in the canyon at that point, and there the pioneer merchant built his store, "an 18 foot square structure that sat diminutive and forlorn at the trail junction." Singer sold supplies to passing army units, buffalo hide freighters, and to the few ranchers in the area.

Beginning in 1883, there were efforts to establish a town in the vicinity of Singer's Store, and by 1890, Old Lubbock, or South Town, had begun to take hold a few miles south of the store. In 1890, Singer moved his place of business to the new town.

In that same year, a man named W.S. Clark ventured out to the South Plains looking for new land for ranching. Clark hailed from Thorp Springs, a small Central Texas community which was the site of Add-Ran College, a church-related school which later evolved into Texas Christian University. Clark had been a student at Add-Ran.

On May 12, 1890, he loaded his family into a covered wagon pulled by a bay mare and a brown mule and set out for the South Plains. The Clark family arrived at its destination near the headwaters of the Brazos on May 24, 1890. A few days later, Clark walked into Old Man Singer's Store and was surprised to meet H.M. Bandy, an old friend from Add-Ran College. Bandy, an itinerant preacher-farmer, had also journeyed to the South Plains in search of inexpensive land and the promise of water.

On the following Sunday, Bandy and the Clark family met at Singer's Store for worship. By the time Bandy stood up to preach that morning, ten other people of various religious faiths had joined the group. That worship service, according to a *History of Lubbock*, was the first church meeting held within the present boundaries of Lubbock. It was also the beginning of what became the Broadway Church of Christ.

Bandy and Clark liked the South Plains so they decided to recruit a colony of Christians from Thorp Springs to join them. Bandy left immediately for his former home where he rounded up forty people, most of them members of the Church of Christ, who agreed to come with him. The caravan of fourteen wagons left Thorp Springs in October, 1890 for the tedious six-week trek to the South Plains. The travelers ended each day with hymns and Bible readings around the camp fire. Each Sunday morning they paused for an hour of worship with the Lord's Supper and sermons by Bandy or one of the other men.

When the Thorp Springs colonists arrived, they found a town which could boast of 37 buildings — and, as one old-timer remarked, fewer people. Among the buildings were Singer's Store, a blacksmith shop, and the Nicolett Hotel, a two-story frame structure whose dining room would serve for the next eight years as the meeting place for Lubbock's embryonic Church of Christ congregation.

Less than a hundred years separate us from those days, and yet those people were living on the frontier. Their religion found congenial soil in which to grow and prosper on the South Plains. They traced their religious origins to the Restoration Movement, an early nineteenth century effort that

sought to break away from the denomina-
tionalism which had fragmented Christianity. Instead of seeking to improve the
denominational system, the leaders of this
movement sought to restore in their worship, organization, and life the pattern of
New Testament Christianity by going back
to the authority of the Scriptures.

At least six distinct Restoration efforts
contributed to today's Disciples of Christ
and the Churches of Christ. One of the most
important was led by Barton W. Stone. In
1802, Stone was suspended from the Presbyterian Church for preaching that all man-
made creeds should be abolished, and that
only the name Christian should be worn.
Nearly 30,000 people in Kentucky and nearby
states responded to Stone's message. Independent groups referring to themselves simply as Christians rose up in Virginia and
North Carolina, in Vermont, and in Indiana.

The most influential Restoration leaders,
Thomas and Alexander Campbell, worked
primarily in western Pennsylvania. Thomas
Campbell, a minister in the Anti-Burgher
Seceder Presbyterian Church in Ireland
came to America in 1807 and broke with the

Presbyterians soon after arriving. He prepared what has been called the "magna charta" of the Restoration Movement, his *Declaration and Address*, a plea for unity based on the belief that the New Testament contained the "blue print and specifications" of the one church. The rule for Campbell's proposed society was "Where the Scriptures speak, we speak; and where the Scriptures are silent, we are silent." This became the watchword for the Restoration Movement.

Thomas Campbell's son, Alexander, preached his first sermon in 1810, and soon became the dominant figure in the Movement (hence the nickname "Campbellites" for Disciples and Churches of Christ members). In 1832, the "Disciples," led by Alexander Campbell, and the "Christians," led by Barton Stone, merged at Lexington, Kentucky. After the union, the Movement experienced tremendous growth, particuarly in the Southeast and Southwest, claiming approximately 350,000 members at the time of Alexander Campbell's death in 1866.

The Disciples, as the Stone-Campbell group came to be called, preached a simple message of Christian unity based on the restoration of the ancient order of things. Membership was based on a five-point "plan of salvation" (Hear, Believe, Repent, Confess, be Baptized) with a distinctive emphasis on immersion for the remission of sins. The Lord's Supper was observed weekly, and the local autonomy of each congregation was maintained under the care of elders and deacons.

A few months after the arrival of this group on the South Plains, the town of Lub-

BROADWAY'S FIRST BUILDING

bock was incorporated — in Febrary, 1891 —
and both the town and the church began to
grow. By 1895, the congregation numbered
about thirty members, with attendance often as high as fifty or seventy-five. In 1898,
the group moved from the Nicolett Hotel to
the county courthouse — with occasional
meetings in the Lubbock jail.

In 1906, the congregation constructed its
first building — a white frame structure, 36'
by 56', with a steeple and a seating capacity
of 300. Local people, eager for the development of any good work to strengthen their
new town, donated the lots for the building
and $1000.

Three years later, the church had become
prosperous enough to hire its first full-time
preacher, a young man named Liff Sanders
who had been preaching part-time for several years.

In 1898, Sanders and his new wife were
living in the little town of Lockney. Sanders
had attended the Nashville Bible School in-
tending to be a preacher, but at the moment
he was working as a cowboy. While visiting
two cousins in Lubbock, he was approached
by church members who asked if he would

consider moving to Lubbock to preach the gospel.

LIFF SANDERS

"I was going to leave Lubbock and go back to Lockney after my visit, and I stopped in the store of J.D. Caldwell," Sanders recalled many years later. "He was the first merchant in Lubbock. I was approached there and told that if I would move to Lubbock, I would be helped in building a house. I came to Lubbock and built a three-room box house. It was in 1900. We were very proud of it. I was the first preacher to make his home in Lubbock. I held my first service in the courthouse."

On that Sunday in 1906 when Sanders preached for the first time in the new church building, cowhands from all around Lubbock rode in on their horses to inspect the new church — and to see if any young ladies were in attendance. They circled the church a couple of times on this fine, sunny Sunday morning and pulled in closer to look in the windows. Sanders, the cowboy preacher, looked out and saw the curious cowpokes. "Come on in, boys," he called out. "We won't hurt you a bit."

Meanwhile, Sanders was still working at other jobs during the week. "Contributions were only fifteen to twenty dollars a month," he recalled. "I had to make a living at the other jobs." He operated a ranch for a while, clerked in a general store, and with a cousin opened a meat market where he recalled selling steak for ten cents a pound and roast for six cents.

In 1909, the year Sanders began preaching full-time, the congregation organized its first Sunday Bible School program. And in 1909, collection plates were for the first time circulated through the audience. As innocuous as it sounds, that was a major break with tradition. Each member had previously been expected to place his individual offering under the white napkin cloth covering the communion table.

Tall, lean Liff Sanders, the cowboy preacher, preached for Broadway until 1919. During the final year of his ministry, church membership had grown to 175. The congregation had a building, a preacher, elders, deacons, and a Sunday School program.

After leaving Broadway, Sanders preached for several West Texas congregations and then moved back to Lubbock in the 1930's. 'Brother Liff' served as a Broadway elder until the 1960's. "He was a remarkable man," Norvel Young recalls. "He earned a lot of respect in the community. He was also a kind man and very understanding to me as one of his successors in the Broadway pulpit."

"One reason that I had the influence with the people that I did in those days," Liff Sanders recalled a few years before he died, "was that I was just one of them. I helped them in everything that came along, and was just one of the citizens of the county. And they looked upon me as such. I helped them fight the prairie fires, and I helped them in whatever came up in the community."

Liff Sanders was a living symbol of Lubbock's and Broadway's rich heritage, and until just a few years ago, several of our members had firsthand knowledge of those beginnings. Now Charlie Collier is one of our last living links with Broadway's early days.

A retired barber and our longest serving elder, Charlie came to Lubbock so long ago he says, "the sun was no bigger than a quarter, and there wasn't no moon."

"All this country was just beginning to be settled," he recalls, and people liked the looks of it, mainly because it was level. We'd have one of these sandstorms, and people would swear they were gonna leave. But they'd wake up the next morning, and it would be a pretty day so they'd stay a little longer."

When Charlie Collier became a Broadway member, Liff Sanders had been succeeded by John T. Smith, a native of Tennessee. Smith brought with him a penchant for organization, and he encouraged the church to keep accurate membership rolls and records on baptisms and business meetings. The church continued to grow during Smith's tenure. By 1920, membership was nearing 250, and contributions averaged close to $70 a week.

In 1921, the congregation began construction on a new brick building on lots purchased at Broadway and Avenue H. The building, with an auditorium seating a thou-

sand was finally completed in 1925, but the first service had been held in the basement three years earlier. Since that long ago Wednesday evening service — on January 26, 1922 — this first church on the South Plains has been known as the Broadway Church of Christ.

John T. Smith was succeeded by T.M. Carney in 1923, R.R. Brooks in 1925, W.M. Davis in 1927, and in 1929, John Smith returned. In 1938, G.C. Brewer, one of the most remarkable men in the brotherhood, came to preach at Broadway.

G.C. Brewer was a handsome, white-haired man with a rhetorical eloquence reminiscent of William Jennings Bryan and a courage that earned him the Carnegie Medal for Heroism. While living in Sherman, Texas he fought off a rabid dog and rescued several children, and with the $5,000 prize he bought a house in Lubbock. In 1928, he had attracted national attention for his lively debate with Judge Ben Lindsay, the articulate free love advocate of that day.

A dedicated Bible scholar, he taught a nondenominational brand of Christianity that kept Broadway out of debilitating sectarian controversies. He continued a Broadway tradition of involvement in Lubbock community affairs and frequently worked in cooperation with other religious groups on matters of mutual concern.

During the Depression, Brewer voluntarily cut his salary in half. According to Mrs. Norvel Young, Mrs. Brewer didn't know her strong-willed husband was going to do that until he had already announced it from the pulpit. "I might have had something to say about it if I had known," Helen Young remembers Mrs. Brewer saying.

Brewer was Broadway's minister for six years before returning to full-time evangelistic work. In Norvel Young's words, "G.C. Brewer helped Broadway catch a worldwide vision of the kingdom; he helped them to be part of a brotherhood." When he resigned in 1943, this pioneer church he had served so well on the isolated South Plains of West Texas in a town of less than 40,000 was poised to become the largest, most influential church in the brotherhood.

**6**

# The Challenge of the City

Broadway's modern era began that day in 1943 when a youthful preacher and his wife arrived by train from Tennessee. They set to work immediately expanding Broadway's involvement on all fronts. Still in their twenties, Norvel and Helen Young weren't accustomed to the flat, treeless prairie around Lubbock — "We didn't know you weren't supposed to visit people during a sandstorm," Helen Young recalls — but soon there was too much to do to think about their arid surroundings. For the next thirteen years missionary activities were increased, benevolent projects started, training series, and youth activities initiated. And just as John T. Smith twenty-five years earlier had successfully rallied sentiment for a new building, Young urged that Broadway build for the future. Our present building, constructed in 1950, is the result.

M. NORVEL YOUNG

Broadway thrived under Norvel Young's leadership, primarily because he was — and is — a man of vision, a man accustomed to the broader view. "It's unbelievable how much you can get done," he once told me, "if you don't care who gets the credit." That comment says something about the man and about his ability to make people feel needed.

Perhaps the program closest to Norvel Young's heart was Broadway's mission effort. In the early 1900's, the church had contributed ten dollars a month toward the support of an evangelist in New Mexico, and there had been partial support for mission work in Japan and other areas, but Broadway's biggest thrust came in the years immediately following World War II.

In 1946, Broadway sent Otis Gatewood to Europe as the first American missionary of any religious group to enter Germany following World War II. Most efforts since then to evangelize Europe can be traced either directly or indirectly to Broadway's beginning.

The European effort was the most extensive and ambitious project Churches of Christ had ever undertaken. It called for Broadway to serve as the sponsoring church in a highly coordinated, carefully planned program involving the fellowship and financial support of scores of smaller sister congregations.

The program was quite successful and attracted the admiration of religious and government leaders on both continents. Hundreds of citizens from our former enemy-nation were baptized into Christ, and most significantly, the program provided the spark and the practical pattern for numerous advances into scores of other unevangelized nations of the world.

The first service was held a year after VE Day in Frankfurt, that city of 500,000 where more than half the homes and buildings had been bombed into destruction. Twenty-two people attended that first service. Attendance subsequently reached 300 a week. Broadway also took the lead in providing approximately $500,000 in food and clothing to the needy of wartime Germany.

Today Broadway continues to support a preaching school in Heidelberg along with mission work in five American cities and eight foreign countries. Over the past few years, those brought to Christ in these mission areas has averaged one person a day.

In 1947, Broadway established the Texas Tech Bible Chair, a pioneering effort under the direction of Carl Spain to serve the rapidly growing student body of what was then Texas Technological College. Today approximately 28,000 college students are receiving their education in Lubbock — 22,000 at Texas Tech University, 1,200 at Lubbock Christian College, and hundreds more in business and vocational schools.

These students are experiencing a whole new dimension of life which is shaping and developing many of their lifetime concepts and beliefs. We believe it is important that

God's people be sensitive to their needs, questions and concerns. But we also believe the universal need of every age — the need for the Good News of Jesus Christ — finds no exception in college students.

On the Tech campus, where the major evangelistic thrust is centered, the college ministry works through a student organization registered with the university called Campus Advance. Campus Advance publishes a newsletter, participates in intramurals, and organizes campus social events and other activities. Student officers work closely with the college ministry staff to coordinate the program.

The Broadway college ministry can best be described in terms of its two purposes. Its primary purpose is evangelistic outreach as it seeks to draw outsiders in to Jesus Christ and the fellowship of Christians. Secondary, but also very important is the purpose of providing strength to Christian collegians whatever their age in Christ. Twelve hundred students on the Tech campus indicate a preference for the Church of Christ, though many have only a loose connection.

The evangelistic outreach through the Bible Chair has seen the conversion of many students. Most were brought to Christ by friends or roommates who first gained their confidence and then studied with them. Many were attracted initially by experiencing the warmth of the Christian fellowship at the Bible Chair. Courses are taught every semester to assist students. Of special significance, in most Tech dorms students are conducting weekly Bible studies in their rooms for groups ranging in number from five to twenty. These groups spark interest and facilitate new friendships which lead to individual studies.

The Bible Chair also offers Bible courses for academic credit. All Tech students are eligible to enroll and can receive elective credit toward their degrees. These courses have drawn many students who might otherwise have had no contact with our students and God's message. The courses are also academically sound, requiring students to really come to grips with what the Bible teaches.

Another Broadway effort owing its origin to Norvel Young's vision is the Children's Home of Lubbock, one of the first child-care agencies to use the concept of cottage-type housing units rather than dormitory-living.

The Children's Home got its start in the early 1950's when Ida S. Collins, member of a pioneer Lubbock family, deeded 200 acres of fertile Panhandle farm land for the site. Ground-breaking ceremonies for the first cottage were held in October, 1953, and the Children's Home opened its doors in April, 1954. Shortly after the first cottage opened, a second one was constructed.

The child-care agency emerging in 1953 was destined to try some concepts not generally practiced in the child-care field in the Southwest at that time. Group care would be given in residential cottages using couples as parents versus the older institutional dormitories characteristic of most group care programs. The multi-service concept brought with it adoptive planning and foster care as options for children. Later the Children's Home of Lubbock would be renamed the Children's Home of Lubbock and Family Service Agency, Inc., and would dedicate its staff and program to a comprehensive family-oriented ministry. Today by design and program, the Children's Home is indeed family-oriented and has an average case load of between 150 and 160 children in care.

According to Tom Burton, the Home's Social Service Administrator, "The programs at the Home are flexible and by design are planned to meet a variety of community and family needs. The Home operates a campus with nine co-educational type cottage units using couples as live-in parents. The campus has a multi-apartment unit for older students designed to give experience in less supervised living."

Five off-campus foster group homes are located in surrounding communities. Two of these operate under contract as emergency shelter units for the Texas Department of Human Resources while the other three operate as group homes for school and adolescent-age youngsters.

With a total operational budget that exceeds $900,000 and with more than two million dollars in debt-free assets and resources, the Children's Home is constantly re-evaluating the type of services it offers. During the sixties, for instance, the Home began to emphasize work with unwed mothers, particularly in adoptive planning. As Superintendent and Administrator Floyd Stumbo points out, "We saw the need because of the change in that area, and now the increased needs of adolescent-age children have caused us to shift from that care. We have always attempted to be an agency that offers to children and their families the best of care available."

Children at the Home — some 1,650 in the past twenty-five years — are served without regard to their race or national origin. They come for a variety of reasons, but generally because of the failure of the family. Their stories are invariably poignant, often heartbreaking, although life at the Home has a way of transforming heartbreaking stories into heartwarming ones. I remember the year of the Charles Manson murders. A young man who had lived in the Home for several years was remarkably similar to Manson in background, age, early experiences, birthdates, and several other areas. The likenesses were striking. But at the time of Manson's atrocities, the young man from the Home was serving in Viet Nam, and at Christmas he sent a check to the Home so that some child would have a nice Christmas. More than one person said it: "If it hadn't been for the Home . . ."

Norvel Young, the architect of so many of this congregation's programs, left Broadway in 1956 to become President of Pepperdine University. (Dr. Young is now Pepperdine's Chancellor.) One of his last major projects at Broadway was to encourage the establishment of Lubbock Christian College. The college opened in 1955 in the Broadway educational building with Broadway elders as its original trustees. Originally a junior college, LCC is now a four-year institution with an enrollment of approximately 1,200 students.

In 1957, George H. Stephenson became Broadway's minister. He served for six years until moving to the South Side congregation in Fort Worth.

In June, 1963, William S. Banowsky came to Broadway. Dr. Banowsky, now President of the University of Oklahoma, brought dynamic, youthful leadership to the church. A forceful, articulate speaker, he became well known for his 1964 debate on the New Morality with Anson Mount of *Playboy Magazine*.

The confrontation attracted an audience of several thousand to the Lubbock Coliseum.

Special programs for the deaf, a jail ministry, programs for the mentally retarded, television and radio ministries, a comprehensive educational program, benevolence efforts, an evangelistic thrust among Spanish-speaking people in Lubbock — this pioneer church has never really stopped pioneering. All these efforts have sprung up over the years in response to needs perceived by a congregation both energetic and innovative.

The Spanish-speaking effort, for instance, grew out of the most devastating disaster in Lubbock history. On the night of May 11, 1970, a killer tornado ripped the heart out of Lubbock. Twenty-three people lost their lives, 500 were injured, and 3,500 were left homeless. Damage was estimated at $135 million.

The American Red Cross immediately set up a clearing and distribution center in our educational annex, and by the end of the week 20,000 meals had been served from our building. Thousands of other persons had received food from the distribution trucks driven into ravaged parts of the city by our people. Thousands of people received clothing from the distribution center in the Broadway building.

Among Lubbock citizens hardest hit by the tornado were thousands of Spanish-speaking people, many of them farm workers who could ill afford any kind of disaster. Through our relief efforts, we got to know our Spanish-speaking neighbors better, and a Spanish-speaking congregation was soon established. Today more than 100 Spanish Christians meet each Sunday in our chapel for worship, and more than 150 children attend special Bible classes.

Today the Broadway Church of Christ is a congregation of some 3,000 members in a rapidly growing city of nearly 200,000 people. The center of what had been an arid, sparsely populated prairie until irrigation water and oil transformed the South Plains into a thriving agricultural and industrial economy, Lubbock is taking advantage of its Sun Belt opportunities. Broadway has literally grown up with the city — is in fact an integral part of the city's fabric — and through the years its membership has included some of Lubbock's most influential people.

The Broadway membership includes numerous successful business executives; numerous farmers; the present city manager (the youngest of a major city in Texas); the woman who heads the Lubbock Civic Center; a Lubbock County Commissioner; and through the years, numerous City Council members. These are people who think in terms of excellence, and their high standards spill over into the work of the Broadway Church as well.

Of course, not everyone at Broadway is a prominent public figure; in fact, some of our most influential members are probably known to few people outside the Broadway family. Their commitment to excellence, however, and their influence for good is just as pervasive as that of their better known brethren, and to know Broadway, it is necessary to know some of them.

I'm thinking of people like Ola Nordyke, an elderly woman so crippled with arthritis she could get around only with great difficulty. From a pioneer Lubbock family, she lived alone in a large old house. Surrounding the house were lovingly tended gardens where she raised flowers of all kinds. For more than thirty years, until her death several years ago, she was the "Flower Lady" at the hospital, slowly making her rounds each week delivering bouquets from her garden to the many patients.

And I think of Ola and Buck Peveto. For twenty-five years, Ola was a supervisor in our Bible School Primary Department, and Buck is a deacon. Until the tornado wiped them out, they ran a small downtown cafe, the Hot Shot Restaurant, across the street from the jail. For years their ministry was to feed for free anyone the church sent to them — and the church sent many.

For ten years Norman Igo was Director of New Construction at Texas Tech. Under his supervision, $250 million in new construction was completed, including a new medical school. On April 30, 1978, Norman Igo resigned.

"As you go through life, you wonder what you can do," Norman told me recently. "I didn't have money and when you preached that sermon on talents, I realized that I had been a member here a long time and had never really put my talents to work. Knowing my talent is managing construction and being as we were successful with the Tech Med School, I got to thinking that this new building would be one place I could put my talents to work."

Norman became construction manager for our building program. Leaving Texas Tech was not easy, he admits; he was well paid, Tech offered a good retirement program, he liked what he was doing. Since taking over our project, however, he has saved us both time and money — an estimated $225,000 in construction costs. "I'm happy with my decision," he says simply.

Carroll Allen, one of our deacons, is a white-haired man in his early sixties with a lop-sided grin and a shy, soft-spoken way about him. A superb wood craftsman, Carroll has made beautiful furnishings for our offices and beautifully crafted items for our Bible School department. He never accepts a fee.

"This is the way I can serve," he once explained. "I know I'll always have a part of this church if some of my things are in it."

Carroll Allen speaks for all of us at Broadway. We are heirs to a proud tradition and like Carroll Allen, we give of ourselves to assure the continuation of that tradition.

That's one reason November 19 did not surprise me.

# 7

# The Challenge to Risk

In a meeting of 1,100 church leaders from several southern states recently, I asked for a show of hands from those who recognized the name Shammua. No hands went up. Shaphat? No hands. Igal? No hands. Palti? Gaddiel? Gaddi? Sethur? Nahbi? Geuel? Somewhere in that list two tentative hands reached about shoulder level so I continued. Joshua? Every hand in the room shot up. Caleb? Hands everywhere — 1,100 of them.

The names, of course, are those of the twelve spies from Israel sent out to infiltrate the land of Canaan. All are listed in the Old Testament, in Numbers 13. But even real students of the Bible could recognize only two — the two men willing to risk.

It was a land flowing with milk and honey, the twelve agreed, but as ten of the spies reported, Canaan is "a land that devours its inhabitants." The people are huge and we felt like grasshoppers, they moaned, pathetic little grasshoppers.

But listen to Joshua and Caleb — the men we remember — as they "rent their clothes" and exhorted their people: "The land which we passed through to spy it out is an exceedingly good land. If the Lord delights in us, he will bring us into this land and give it to us, a land which flows with milk and honey. Only do not rebel against the Lord; do not fear the people of the land, for they are bread for us; their protection is removed from them and the Lord is with us; do not fear them."

The people of Israel answered Joshua and Caleb with a hail of stones, and because they would not listen, because they were afraid to risk, they spent forty years wandering in a desolate wilderness.

In the New Testament, the apostle Peter, good old impetuous Peter, is almost the embodiment of risk. Out on a treacherous sea late at night with his fellow disciples, Peter sees his Master walking across the water toward the boat. Peter clambers over the side, and miraculously, he too walks on the water — until the wind terrifies him and he begins to sink.

As Bonhoeffer observes, "Peter had to leave the ship and risk his life on the sea, in order to learn both his own weakness and the almightly power of his Lord. If Peter had not taken the risk, he would never have learnt the meaning of his faith." (*Cost of Discipleship*, p. 68)

Looking back over Broadway's past, it seems to me that everything significant Broadway has accomplished — beginning with those forty-one people who left their homes and journeyed to the South Plains and continuing through our record-breaking contribution — has involved risk. Elders who commit themselves to constructing a $3.8 million building and members who contribute more than they ever dreamed possible are taking risks. But like Peter, we take the risk to learn the meaning of our faith.

Risk-taking, however, grows progressively more difficult as an individual, as an organization, grows older. Talking with a group of elders recently, I pointed out that in their businesses they couldn't afford to take the risks now that they took as younger men. Now they have achieved some stability, and they cannot afford to throw it all on the line. When they were younger, if they lost it all, they still had time to recoup.

"I never really thought about it," one of the elders, a doctor, said to me afterward, "but fifteen years ago, I owed a million dollars. There's no way I could take that risk today."

"Every growing organism," wrote Dewey and Dakin, "grows to maturity, levels off and dies unless there is new life . . . new blood . . . new ideas and . . . new activity." Churches are no exception. They usually grow old like people, get tired, get sick, and die.

Whereas death is inevitable for a person, it is not, however, for a church — as Dewey and Dakin's comments about new life, new blood, new ideas, and new activity would suggest. What often happens though is that men who lead churches grow older and tend to think of the church in the same terms they think of their businesses or their personal lives. They want to be solvent in their businesses; they want to be solvent in their personal lives. And, as responsible stewards, they want the church to be in good business shape as well.

Solvency, of course, is a worthy aim, but when it comes to the church, we're in another realm, the realm of faith. And as Peter discovered, faith demands that we step out and take the risk. Whenever a church becomes so totally business-like that it depends on its own strength and never leans on God, that is the beginning of the end.

Amen!, we shout, and yet caution frequently rears its tempting — and responsible head. "We've got this church paid for; we've got it all done; we've built all we're going to; we've got all the property we're going to need" — very persuasive arguments, or at least they can be, for a church, particularly for a congregation the age of Broadway. "Let's get this taken care of so that our children won't have to build anything" — that's another one, and very persuasive too, and yet that argument represents one of the most attractively disguised stumbling blocks I can imagine for our children. They too need to build, to plan, to risk.

With tomorrow's Broadway in mind, I have mixed emotions, for example, in regard to our deferred gifts program. As we discussed in a preceding chapter, I firmly believe that a person who has invested his life in this church should be able to will his money to the church at his death; and yet I just as firmly believe we must avoid becoming an endowed church. A well known church in New York City, for instance, is endowed; its leaders need never ask its members for anything. Some of the most powerful preachers in the nation have tried — and failed — to build that church — in my opinion, *because* it is endowed. When nothing is demanded of a people, nothing is built.

If significant wills come our way, I would recommend a policy that would earmark all such money for mission work, benevolence, and other outside activities. The money should not be used to endow the ongoing local program of the church. That takes all the risk out.

But how does a church, particularly an older church, maintain that youthful vigor that welcomes risk, that "tests God?"

One vital necessity is to groom leaders — elders, deacons, teachers, and staff — who are not afraid to risk. We're not talking about a man who is rash, reckless, impetuous; we're talking about one who does his homework, who builds a strong, carefully considered case. Eventually, however, this leader must take the leap into the unknown with a willingness to risk everything to make the dream reality. He must also be able to inspire others to take the leap. That's leadership.

And that is why there are few real leaders. There are thousands of people who must remain in secondary positions because they are afraid to risk. Fearful of the consequences if plans go awry, they must forever remain in the shadows. The real leader, on the other hand, is courageous — not foolhardy, but courageous. He makes the decision and calls the play, accepting all the consequences. He is strong, willing to say — to borrow Harry Truman's pithy phrase — "The buck stops here."

No church can maintain growth larger than the vision of its leadership. Unusual circumstances — a rapidly growing area, an aggressive preacher — may cause a spurt of growth, but a church will inevitably level out at the top of its leadership's vision. Leadership whose vision tops out at 500 members will keep its congregation at that level or below. Leadership whose vision tops out at 1000 members will keep its congregation at that level — regardless of the opportunity level of the church.

As we have seen in preceding chapters, Broadway's leadership has been a key ingredient in her growth. The reason Broadway has had a constant growth pattern for nearly a century is precisely because her leaders have had vision.

Over the years, Broadway's elders have taken great pains to employ capable people — and to give them freedom to do the job the way they were hired to do. A good leader, of course, surrounds himself with people who know more than he does about certain things. An insecure man will always have trouble being a good leader because he will surround himself with inferior men who pose no threat to his leadership position. Big men are always a threat to little men.

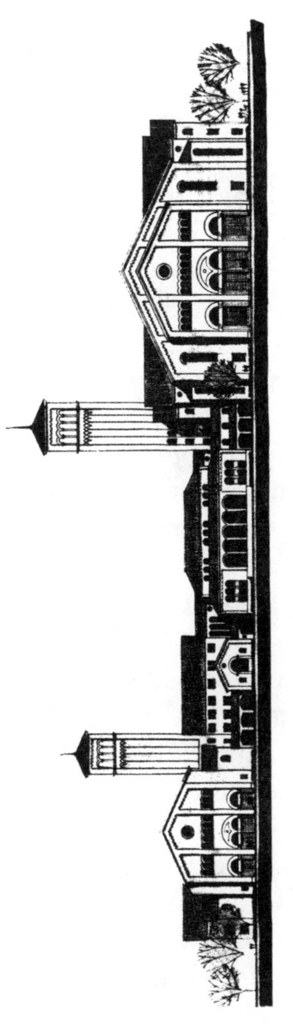

BROADWAY CHURCH OF CHRIST — LONG RANGE DEVELOPMENT PLAN

Broadway's elders have employed people in whom they have confidence and let them do their job. Responsibility without authority places one in an impossible situation, so our elders give people big responsibilities and the authority to fulfill them.

Broadway has had only ten pulpit preachers. They too have been men of vision who stayed long enough to do the job. They have been men who were powerful in the pulpit, but their work extended beyond that. They dreamed great dreams, and they were given the freedom to implement those dreams. Most of them have belonged not just to this congregation but to the brotherhood at large, and they lent their influence to good works everywhere. That expanded vision enriched their work at Broadway.

Broadway's leaders have made mistakes at times — sometimes big ones. But as our November 19 contribution reaffirmed, they have not yet made the biggest mistake of all — the mistake of doing nothing because of indecisiveness. The French author Andre Gide put it this way many years ago: "Man cannot discover new oceans unless he has courage to lose sight of the shore."

# The Challenge to Go Forward

"One of the most exciting ideas that has ever entered my mind," Elton Trueblood writes in *The Future of the Christian*, "is that we are living in the early days of the Christian faith. We are early Christians!" Trueblood goes on to affirm his conviction that "God has purposes for this world which are not yet fulfilled and man can be his instrument in working for their fulfillment."

I'm inspired by that idea too, and it makes me realize that we are early Christians at Broadway for sure — ninety years is not really very long. As we look to the future we can see much waiting to be done. To again borrow Trueblood's inspiring words, and to bring them home to Lubbock, "It is our opportunity not merely to restore the Christian faith, and not merely to maintain it, but to guide it into new channels."

In the immediate future, we look forward to occupying our new building sometime in the summer of 1980. At this point, we need $1,400,000 to walk through the doors of that building debt-free; the gifts are still coming, and with the sacrificial spirit of our people, we're confident we'll make it.

The building, we believe, allows God to continue using us in ever-expanding ministries. It will include a library, for example, which will contain resource materials to aid Christian growth. It will include the Historical Center, housing an impressive collection of historical memorabilia relating to the Broadway Church; the Conference Center, providing much-needed space for elders' meetings; and the Garden Center, a multi-purpose area for weddings, receptions, exhibits, special meetings, Bible classes, lounge and fellowship area. The new building will also offer additional space for nursery, preschool, and adult Bible classes.

Taking a longer range view of the future, we can see several areas that need attention. An obvious gap we need to fill is ministry to the elderly. We have superb programs for children, for young people, for college students, but nothing specific for our older members — which seems ironic for a church so conscious of its rich heritage. What form a ministry to the elderly will take we are not yet sure, but it's important that we provide our older members opportunities to minister as well as opportunities to be ministered to. They've got time, they've got heart, and this congregation needs their talents and experience.

We also expect to increase our use of media, both print and electronic. "Go into all the world and preach the gospel to the whole creation" (Mark 16:15). Our mandate is clear. Our primary obligation is to preach the gospel to those who do not know Jesus. With a world population of over four billion souls, the task calls for bold, fearless use of every tool available to get that job done. It isn't sufficient for us to wait for people to come to our building before we approach them with the message of salvation. To reach the greatest number of people we must use the media — radio, television, and printed page.

At present, Broadway produces two local radio programs. The Lubbock Bible Class, an outreach class that I teach, is broadcast live each Sunday morning. Designed with the non-Christian in mind, we make every effort to "involve" the listener — by offering to mail free materials to listeners, by maintaining contact with those who write or call, and by seeking to gain the confidence of the listening audience. Results have been gratifying.

We also broadcast live the Sunday evening service of the Broadway church. We have a large audience and many regular listeners tune us in from hundreds of miles away.

Our television ministry is a local, studio-produced program called "A Better Life" aired each Sunday morning at 11:00. The thirty-minute program consists of Bible messages, interviews, and music. The program has enjoyed high ratings, pulling the largest audience of any locally produced religious program; in fact, "A Better Life" provides Broadway with the largest audience of any ministry of the congregation.

*Pathway Evangelism* is a nonprofit organization established to distribute religious literature to non-Christians. Based on the idea that non-Christians will not subscribe to our religious journals, we send them teaching materials free of charge. Three times each month printed messages are sent to thousands of people, with funds for the ministry being contributed by those interested in getting these "paper missionaries" into the homes of non-Christians. Conversions are coming weekly from this growing ministry.

The philosophy behind all our media ministries is that when a person meets a crisis in his life, he is going to turn for help to those who have exhibited sufficient interest to use radio, television, and the printed page to get his attention. We're using media, but we need to use them even more extensively.

We must also be conscious of special areas in which we can develop ministries. This congregation was the first in our brotherhood, for example, to hire an educational minister (Alan. M. Bryan in 1952), and we ought to be the first to hire full-time supervisors at each level of our educational program. We're moving in that direction.

But the programs we plan today, as important as they are, will no doubt be inadequate for tomorrow's needs. That's to be expected. To serve effectively, we must be flexible, ready to move quickly wherever we are needed. Like a well coached, triple-option quarterback, we must be ready to use the most effective weapon in our arsenal, depending on the situation.

Years ago someone came up with the idea that every church ought to formulate a TEN-YEAR PLAN. Most churches came up with such a plan — and in some cases it set the church *back* ten years. Why?

Goals and plans are important, and should propel a church forward, but the problem was that no flexibility was built into the plan. Consequently, when the church came up against obstacles two years deep into the program, the only alternative seemed to be to abandon the plan. It was a terribly negative, devastating experience. Had some flexibility been included in the plan, it wouldn't have happened.

The need for flexibility exists in every

area of church life  There should be flexibility in buildings, for instance. Today you may have large, open spaces; tomorrow you may want small classrooms. Flexibility in methods and areas of ministry is even more vital. And there should be flexibility in goals. We don't give up on goals simply because we encounter roadblocks. At times it may become necessary to detour, but if we are flexible we need never lose sight of our goals.

Another quality we will continue to cultivate is that of balance, that delicate state of equilibrium indispensible to any effectively functioning organism or institution. The gospel writer Luke was describing balance when he wrote that "Jesus increased in wisdom and in stature, and in favor with God and man" (Luke 2:52). Balance is important in every area of life — though difficult to achieve — and it is absolutely essential in a healthy, growing church. When a church builds on a single program, the whole thing crumbles if that one program fails.

Some churches, for example, major in mission work and ignore local work; some are interested solely in local affairs and ignore missions. Some emphasize benevolence and exclude missions or *vice versa*. Some are strongly evangelistic and ignore edification while some are all edification and no evangelism. Some build youth programs and ignore the elderly while others emphasize the opposite. Some insist that the only way to learn is through small-group discussions while others completely refuse small groups in favor of large lecture classes.

We could go on, but the point is that a balanced church is not going to ignore any potentially useful ideas or activities. People in a congregation have varied interests, of course, and wise church leaders will encourage those interests while at the same time insuring that they do not compete with each other.

Several years ago I started trying to persuade our elders to take several special contributions each year. They were understandably reluctant, feeling that special contributions would in effect be competition with ourselves. I argued that people who give to one special contribution, because it's the area of their interest, aren't going to give substantially to other special contributions anyway.

We now have three or four special contributions each year, and each one brings from $5,000 to $50,000. At the same time, our regular budget has risen from $268,000 in 1968 to more than $1,000,000 this year.

We've learned that many of our people will give to each special contribution. Others are more selective. A balanced congregation can tolerate, even encourage, those special interests without slighting any of them.

I'm excited about Broadway's future. There is much to do, but the vitality, the resources, and the will are available in abundance. When I think about the challenges — indeed the risks — that lie ahead, I often remember Raleigh Martin, a man who served as an elder at Broadway from 1912 until the 1960's. He was attending elders' meetings when he was nearly ninety. He couldn't hear too well, but before adjourning their meetings, the elders always asked him if he had anything to say. Unfailingly, Raleigh Martin's response was, "Brethren, let's go forward."

Where will the Broadway Church of Christ be in five years, in ten years? No one knows for sure, of course, but assuming that

Lubbock doesn't run out of water, that West Texas doesn't run out of cattle and oil, and that our people don't run out of faith and vision, we have much to look forward to. We are praying for the vision to use whatever circumstances surround us as an opportunity to proclaim the Lord's salvation. And joining hands with God, we are encouraging each other with Raleigh Martin's words: "Brethren, let's go forward!"